Flickering
God
The Father

Noel and Denise Enete

WAVE
Study
Bible

Published by WAVE Study Bible, Inc., *wavestudybible.com*
Available from Amazon, *amazon.com*
Edition 1.0.0

(c) Copyright Dr. Noel Enete and Dr. Denise Enete, 2007-2024

All rights reserved.
No part of this book may be reproduced,
stored in a retrieval system, or transmitted in any form, without
the written permission of Dr. Noel Enete and Dr. Denise Enete.

Scripture quotations noted **NIV** are taken from the HOLY BIBLE, NEW INTERNATIONAL VERSION. Copyright 1973, 1978, and 1984 by International Bible Society. Used by permission of Zondervan Publishing House. All rights reserved.

Scripture quotations noted **NASB** are taken from the NEW AMERICAN STANDARD BIBLE, Copyright 1960, 1962, 1963, 1968, 1971, 1972, 1973, 1975, 1977, by The Lockman Foundation. Used by permission.

The FLCR study strategy was adapted from Anne Graham Lotz's *Living a Life that is Blessed*, Copyright 1995 by AnGel Ministries.

ISBN 978-0-9791595-7-2

Printed and bound in the United States of America

Table of Contents

Preface   5

   Organization of the Book

   How To Flicker the Bible

   Example: Psalm 121

1—God Involves Us (Exodus 3:9-22)   12

2—Asking For Reassurance (Judges 6:34-40)   18

3—Asking For Wisdom (1 Kings 3:1-14)   26

4—God Is A Team Player (John 6:36-40)   34

5—Facing Sin (2 Samuel 24:9-19)   40

6—Help In Unlikely Places (1 Kings 17:7-16)   48

7—God's Broad Shoulders (Ezekiel 36:21-32)   54

8—Love Your Enemies (Matthew 5:43-48)   60

"Let him who boasts boast of this, that he understands and knows Me"

Jeremiah 9:24 (NASB1995)

Preface

God wants to be known.

We are *His* children living in *His* creation. He has definite plans and purposes for us so He has made Himself knowable. Knowing Him is the one thing He wants us to be able to boast about.

But how can we get to know God?

We get to know people by watching them and we can get to know God the same way. When we watch people we see what they care about, what makes them happy, sad, or joyful.

We can watch God the same way.

God has revealed Himself in the Bible and we can watch what He does to see what moves Him, what He values, and what He disdains. He reveals this to us and invites us to join Him.

In these eight passages from the Bible notice what He cares about, what moves Him, what He values, and what He gets emotional about. God shows us these things in His Word and knowing *Him* is truly something to boast about.

Organization of the Book

This book takes you through several passages that show what moves God the Father—what He loves, what makes Him sad, and how He is always faithful.

The format of this book encourages you to write out what you notice in the passages and respond to God accordingly. Then as you explore these passages, also be alert to notice what you can learn about what God is like.

If you are not familiar with *Flicker Bible Study*, an explanation of the steps and an example of a *Flickered* passage follows.

How To Flicker the Bible

Facts

In the *Facts* panel, make a list of the *Facts* you see in the passage. You don't have to list all the details. Just try and find the main points. You can use the same words as are in the passage. You will usually get somewhere around four to six *Facts*.

Lessons

In the *Lessons* panel, look over the list of facts and see what you can learn from the passage.

- Is there an example to follow?
- Is there a behavior to stop or start?
- Is there a comfort to accept?

Also, consider what you can learn about God from this passage? What does He value? What does He respond to? What pleases Him? You don't have to find a *Lesson* from every verse. Usually you will get one or two *Lessons* from a passage.

Challenges

In the *Challenges* panel, turn each *Lesson* you surfaced into a question that *Challenges* you. Listen for God to speak to you. He may not speak to you through every verse, but He will speak to you. You will normally get the same number of *Challenges* as *Lessons*.

Response

In the *Response* panel, consider what God is saying to you through this passage and decide how you will respond. Write out your *Response* as a two or three sentence prayer.

Be heartfelt and honest with God. If needed, put "training wheels" on your *Response*: "Lord help me to want this." Better to be honest and ask for help, than promise behavior you are not ready to keep.

Example: Psalm 121

To get an idea how to fill in the panels, the following pages present *Psalm 121 Flickered*. This is a guide to help you understand what kind of item goes in each panel.

More items are included in each panel than you would normally write out in the study of a passage. More are included to give you a better idea what goes in each panel.

For more explanation of *Flicker Bible Study* see our book, *Flickering the Bible: Desire-powered Inductive Bible Study*.

Example Passage

Psalms 121:1 I lift up my eyes to the mountains; From where shall my help come?

Psalms 121:2 My help [comes] from the LORD, Who made heaven and earth.

Psalms 121:3 He will not allow your foot to slip; He who keeps you will not slumber.

Psalms 121:4 Behold, He Who keeps Israel Will neither slumber nor sleep.

Psalms 121:5 The LORD is your keeper; the LORD is your shade on your right hand;

Psalms 121:6 The sun will not smite you by day, Nor the moon by night.

Psalms 121:7 The LORD will protect you from all evil; He will keep your soul.

Psalms 121:8 The Lord will guard your going out and your coming in From this time forth and forever. (NASB)

FLCR FACTS

I look up and wonder where my help will come from.

My help comes from God who made heaven and earth

God won't let me fall because He is always watching. He doesn't sleep

He keeps Israel and doesn't sleep or even slumber

The Lord keeps me and shades me at my right hand

The Lord protects me from evil He is keeping my soul safe

FLCR LESSONS

There are times we know we need help beyond ourselves

Help comes from God Who created heaven and earth and is alert and ready to help

God is constantly watching, ready to catch me before I fall

He can be so attentive because He never sleep or slumbers

God "keeps" Israel; God "keeps" me. Keeping me means He observes me, guards me, takes care of me, maintains me, retains me in His possession.

FLCR CHALLENGES

Am I humble enough to seek help when I need it?

Do I go to God for help, or something else?

Do I trust God to "keep" me?

Am I willing to learn what God considers "falling" instead of assuming falling means failure.

FLCR RESPONSES

Lord, help me to be more aware of Your help and presence.

Help me see my relationship with You from Your perspective.

Passage 1—God Involves Us (Exodus 3:9-22)

Exodus 3:9 "Now, behold, the cry of the sons of Israel has come to Me; furthermore, I have seen the oppression with which the Egyptians are oppressing them.

Exodus 3:10 "Therefore, come now, and I will send you to Pharaoh, so that you may bring My people, the sons of Israel, out of Egypt."

Exodus 3:11 But Moses said to God, "Who am I, that I should go to Pharaoh, and that I should bring the sons of Israel out of Egypt?"

Exodus 3:12 And He said, "Certainly I will be with you, and this shall be the sign to you that it is I who have sent you: when you have brought the people out of Egypt, you shall worship God at this mountain."

Exodus 3:13 Then Moses said to God, "Behold, I am going to the sons of Israel, and I will say to them, 'The God of your fathers has sent me to you.' Now they may say to me, 'What is His name?' What shall I say to them?"

Exodus 3:14 God said to Moses, "I AM WHO I AM"; and He said, "Thus you shall say to the sons of Israel, 'I AM has sent me to you.'"

Exodus 3:15 God, furthermore, said to Moses, "Thus you shall say to the sons of Israel, 'The LORD, the God of your fathers, the God of Abraham, the God of Isaac, and the God of Jacob, has sent me to you.' This is My name forever, and this is My memorial-name to all generations.

Exodus 3:16 "Go and gather the elders of Israel together and say to them, 'The LORD, the God of your fathers, the God of Abraham, Isaac and Jacob, has appeared to me, saying, "I am indeed concerned about you and what has been done to you in Egypt.

Exodus 3:17 "So I said, I will bring you up out of the affliction of Egypt to the land of the Canaanite and the Hittite and the Amorite and the Perizzite and the Hivite and the Jebusite, to a land flowing with milk and honey."'

Exodus 3:18 "They will pay heed to what you say; and you with the elders of Israel will come to the king of Egypt and you will say to him, 'The LORD, the God of the Hebrews, has met with us. So now, please, let us go a three days' journey into the wilderness, that we may sacrifice to the LORD our God.'

Exodus 3:19 "But I know that the king of Egypt will not permit you to go, except under compulsion.

Exodus 3:20 "So I will stretch out My hand and strike Egypt with all My miracles which I shall do in the midst of it; and after that he will let you go.

Exodus 3:21 "I will grant this people favor in the sight of the Egyptians; and it shall be that when you go, you will not go empty-handed.

Exodus 3:22 "But every woman shall ask of her neighbor and the woman who lives in her house, articles of silver and articles of gold, and clothing; and you will put them on your sons and daughters. Thus you will plunder the Egyptians." (NASB1995)

FLCR FACTS

God hears the cry of the sons of Israel.

FLCR **LESSONS**

Sometimes God has to compel a person to comply with His will.

FLCR CHALLENGES

Am I willing to comply with God's will so He doesn't have to compel me?

FLCR RESPONSES

Commentary

Most of us tend to be like Moses, stuck on the question, "who am I?" But God wants us to be stuck on the question, "what do You want me to do?" Our life would change dramatically if we focused on His ability instead of our limitations! When you suffer, what do you tell yourself? Do you tell yourself that God cares about your pain and wants to deliver you to a good situation? That would be in line with the truth in this passage. But what if He asks you to do something outside your comfort zone to get there? Many of us would rather stick with our current suffering because we know it, rather than risk stepping into the unknown.

God saw the Israelites being oppressed by the Egyptians and picked Moses to lead them out. Moses had expressed interest in the Israelites' plight 30 years earlier when he took matters into his own hands and killed an Egyptian *(Exodus 2:11-12)*. God sidelined Moses for 30 years until Moses wasn't feeling so self-adequate. Now he knows he needs to rely on God. Perfect! God uses ordinary people to use His power to do extraordinary things. He is concerned about our pain and suffering, and wants to deliver us into good situations. But sometimes God has to wait until we are ready to choose Him over our own ability.

God's Name is important to Him and to us. God's Name is "I AM" and it is expansive. "I AM" is complete. He is not "becoming," He "is." As His children we are all in process—we are "becoming." But He is complete—He "is." That is why He wants to be remembered by this name (the Hebrew form of this Name is YHWH). He wants us to remember how He dealt with our forefathers because He never changes and will deal with us the same way. His Name represents our Father Who is, present tense. He is always there for us, like He was always there for them.

When God asks us to do something difficult, He often foretells what will happen to encourage us. He knew this was a stretch for Moses, so He told Him what to expect. Everything He predicted came true. Because Moses was willing to step out of his comfort zone and follow God, Moses has been revered to this day in all three major religions: Christianity, Judaism, and Islam.

God deals with us in the same manner. He asks us to do some difficult things and He gives us a good sense of what we can expect through prophecies and promises in His Word. He also encourages us with the promise of rewards. Just imagine what rewards could be ours if we only focused on His promise, "certainly I will be with you."

What God is Like

- *1. God is confident.* He can use fallible children to accomplish His will.
- *2. God is encouraging.* He demonstrated His power to Moses by appearing to him in fire before He asked Moses to do something scary.
- *3. God is concerned about His children's pain.*
- *4. God respects authority.* He has Moses deal with Pharaoh. He could have ordered the Israelites to leave without Pharaoh's permission.
- *5. God wants His children to have nice things.*

Passage 2—Asking For Reassurance (Judges 6:34-40)

Judges 6:34 So the Spirit of the LORD came upon Gideon; and he blew a trumpet, and the Abiezrites were called together to follow him.

Judges 6:35 He sent messengers throughout Manasseh, and they also were called together to follow him; and he sent messengers to Asher, Zebulun, and Naphtali, and they came up to meet them.

Judges 6:36 Then Gideon said to God, "If You will deliver Israel through me, as You have spoken,

Judges 6:37 behold, I will put a fleece of wool on the threshing floor. If there is dew on the fleece only, and it is dry on all the ground, then I will know that You will deliver Israel through me, as You have spoken."

Judges 6:38 And it was so. When he arose early the next morning and squeezed the fleece, he drained the dew from the fleece, a bowl full of water.

Judges 6:39 Then Gideon said to God, "Do not let Your anger burn against me that I may speak once more; please let me make a test once more with the fleece, let it now be dry only on the fleece, and let there be dew on all the ground."

Judges 6:40 God did so that night; for it was dry only on the fleece, and dew was on all the ground. (NASB1995)

FLCR FACTS

Gideon talked to God.

FLCR LESSONS

God can equip us to do His will, and we can still need reassurance.

FLCR CHALLENGES

Am I willing to believe that God will equip me to do His will?

FLCR RESPONSES

Commentary

Gideon started out great! God's Spirit came upon him to equip him to deliver Israel. He was confident. He blew a trumpet to have the Abiezrites follow him. In his enthusiasm he sent messengers to several territories so thousands came ready to fight for Israel.

Then enter Gideon's insecurity. He started worrying that he was imagining things. "Did God really say He would deliver Israel through me? Maybe I'm going to look really foolish and delusional."

So he devises a plan to make sure he wasn't going to misunderstand God's will. After all, this was a BIG deal, leading a whole country into battle. God understood what a BIG thing He was asking, so God cooperated with Gideon's insecurity.

To Gideon's credit, he goes to God for reassurance about His will. He does not go to the army for their opinion, or ask his family if he is crazy. He goes to God and devises a foolproof "flipping of the coin" plan. Wet fleece we go, dry fleece we stay. Sure enough the fleece is wet, so we go. Gulp.

Ok, Lord, best out of two. Please don't get mad. Dry fleece we go, wet fleece we stay.

So the fleece was dry—confirmation, he was not crazy or delusional. He worked it out with God. He was willing to go now. I don't think God minds if we wrestle with Him a bit when He is asking us to do something BIG and we want some reassurance from HIM. We can see God's patience and kindness in these seven verses.

Now, if we studied the rest of the story we would see even more about our Heavenly Father.

For example, we would see more evidence that God understands our weakness. In Gideon's excitement he sent out many messengers and recruited thousands of warriors. I'm sure that boosted Gideon's confidence as he looked at the strength of their numbers. But, God wanted to strengthen their confidence in Him, not their confidence in themselves. He spells this out in the next chapter: *"Israel would become boastful, saying, 'My own power has delivered me.'" (Judges 7:2 NASB1995)*

So God sent home, without shame, anyone who was afraid to fight (22,000 men). The 10,000 men who remained were still too many. Out of those God tells Gideon to pick the 300 men who drank water from their hands instead of putting their face in the stream to drink. (Maybe these 300 were the most aware of their surroundings and would be the most skilled at combat.) Then Gideon sends everyone else home.

He has his small army now. That night God tells him to attack because God has already given Gideon and the Israelites the victory!

God sees Gideon's fear *but He does not get exasperated*. He accommodates and works around Gideon's fear. He tells Gideon that if he is afraid, he should take his servant and go to the enemy's camp and listen. He will be greatly encouraged.

At the enemy camp God gives one of the enemy soldiers a dream that Gideon will have victory over them! Even though their armies are like swarms of locusts and their camels are too many to count, they believe the dream that they will lose and were fearful! As a result of seeing this Gideon's confidence was boosted.

Now Gideon is ready for battle. He divides the 300 into 3 groups and uses them to surround the enemy camp. They blow their trumpets and hold blazing torches and shout. Then they watch as God causes the enemy to rush around in panic killing each other.

Gideon was a flawed man, but God worked His will through an insecure but receptive sinner.

We need God too and He is willing to help us find a way to depend on Him. He doesn't get exasperated by our insecurities, He finds a way to accommodate them if we are wanting to do His will.

What God is Like

- 1. *He wants us to join Him in accomplishing His will.*
- 2. *He wants to help us do His will.*
- 3. *He wants us to trust Him.*
- 4. *He is patient.*
- 5. *He can work with imperfection and still accomplish His will.*
- 6. *He is humble.* He accommodated Gideon's need for reassurance. He did not proudly get offended and incensed.
- 7. *He is sovereignly in control.* He can cause a dream and control the timing of retelling it out loud.
- 8. *He can cause evil to panic and destroy themselves.*
- 9. *He does not need us to help Him be victorious, but He shares His glory with us.*
- 10. *He is loyal to His people even when we don't deserve it.*
- 11. *He chooses to work with His children to accomplish His work.*
- 12. *He guides us in a gentle and understanding way.*
- 13. *God loves to do the impossible for us to show us His power.*

"God doesn't mind giving reassurance for the big things."

the Authors

Passage 3—Asking For Wisdom (1 Kings 3:1-14)

1 Kings 3:1 Then Solomon formed a marriage alliance with Pharaoh king of Egypt, and took Pharaoh's daughter and brought her to the city of David until he had finished building his own house and the house of the LORD and the wall around Jerusalem.

1 Kings 3:2 The people were still sacrificing on the high places, because there was no house built for the name of the LORD until those days.

1 Kings 3:3 Now Solomon loved the LORD, walking in the statutes of his father David, except he sacrificed and burned incense on the high places.

1 Kings 3:4 The king went to Gibeon to sacrifice there, for that was the great high place; Solomon offered a thousand burnt offerings on that altar.

1 Kings 3:5 In Gibeon the LORD appeared to Solomon in a dream at night; and God said, "Ask what [you wish] Me to give you."

1 Kings 3:6 Then Solomon said, "You have shown great lovingkindness to Your servant David my father, according as he walked before You in truth and righteousness and uprightness of heart toward You; and You have reserved for him this great lovingkindness, that You have given him a son to sit on his throne, as [it is] this day.

1 Kings 3:7 "Now, O LORD my God, You have made Your servant king in place of my father David, yet I am but a little child; I do not know how to go out or come in.

1 Kings 3:8 "Your servant is in the midst of Your people which You have chosen, a great people who are too many to be numbered or counted.

1 Kings 3:9 "So give Your servant an understanding heart to judge Your people to discern between good and evil. For who is able to judge this great people of Yours?"

1 Kings 3:10 It was pleasing in the sight of the Lord that Solomon had asked this thing.

1 Kings 3:11 God said to him, "Because you have asked this thing and have not asked for yourself long life, nor have asked riches for yourself, nor have you asked for the life of your enemies, but have asked for yourself discernment to understand justice,

1 Kings 3:12 behold, I have done according to your words. Behold, I have given you a wise and discerning heart, so that there has been no one like you before you, nor shall one like you arise after you.

1 Kings 3:13 "I have also given you what you have not asked, both riches and honor, so that there will not be any among the kings like you all your days.

1 Kings 3:14 "If you walk in My ways, keeping My statutes and commandments, as your father David walked, then I will prolong your days." (NASB1995)

FLCR FACTS

Solomon formed a marriage alliance with Pharaoh's daughter.

FLCR LESSONS

Sometimes God uses dreams to speak to us.

FLCR CHALLENGES

Do I pay attention to vivid, unusual dreams?

FLCR RESPONSES

Commentary

It is interesting to note that Solomon was not behaving perfectly when God blessed him. The chapter starts off mentioning the political alliance Solomon made by marrying Pharaoh's daughter. God told them clearly and repeatedly not to marry foreign women *(e.g. Deuteronomy 7:3-4)* because they would bring in their foreign gods. As it turns out, marrying a multitude of foreign women with their foreign gods was Solomon's downfall by the end of his life.

On the other hand, what Solomon was doing right, was loving God and wanting to walk in the statutes of his father David. But, David had made it a point to get rid of the high places (pagan places of idol worship). God was tolerant of Solomon using a high place to offer worship to Him. God is not legalistic.

It is not surprising that Solomon's extravagant gift touched God's heart. God is a Giver who looks for opportunities to help and give. So He came to Solomon in a dream and told him to ask for whatever he wanted.

In the dream Solomon starts out being grateful for what God had already done through his father David. He acknowledged he was king because God was blessing David through him.

But, Solomon also wanted something. He humbly admitted that he is not equipped to reign well (he was just a child). So He asked for wisdom to rule over God's great nation. Notice Solomon's humility—it was God's great nation, not his, and he felt inadequate.

This pleases God! God longs to work with us and enable us so we can do His will! He not only made Solomon wise, but wiser than anyone before or after him! And God is not done giving! He gives to us more than we could ever ask, or think, as we love and obey Him *(Ephesians 3:20)*.

God loved Solomon's unselfish prayer. It was a servant's prayer to ask to serve well. He didn't ask for spectacular riches, honor, long life, or the life of his enemies. So God gave him spectacular riches and honor as bonus gifts.

He also offered Solomon another blessing of long life if he was willing to obey the way his father David obeyed. David did not obey perfectly so the bar was set realistically.

It is interesting that God gave him riches and honor but did not offer the other thing he could have asked for—the life of his enemies. Apparently, God did not want to kill Solomon's enemies. God loved them and wanted to give them a chance to turn to Him.

What David did best was he kept a sincere and loving heart for God even after dramatically failing Him. Solomon also starts out with his heart attuned to God. And God was pleased. God knew Solomon would fail, but He didn't hold that against him in the present.

God knows we need Him. He is hoping we also know we need Him and that we walk accordingly. Both David and Solomon had hearts for God, but feet of clay. Fortunately, God has a soft spot for our weak tendency to sin. He has made provision to forgive us. But He is moved by our extravagant love and grateful response.

What God is Like

- *1. God is more focused on our loving heart for Him, than our sinlessness.*
- *2. God WANTS to give to us more than we can imagine.*
- *3. God WANTS to help and enable us.*
- *4. God WANTS us to know Him and sometimes communicates to us through dreams.*
- *5. God does NOT hold a grudge.* He forgives as we confess. He forgave David and continued to bless him after his death.

- *6. God does not withhold current blessings even when He knows we will fail him later.*
- *7. God is flexible.* He accepted genuine worship in a high place. David and Solomon had different opinions on using the high places for worship and God accepted them both.
- *8. God is moved by extravagant giving to Him because He is an extravagant Giver to us.* He wants us to be like Him.
- *9. God is our Source of wisdom.*
- *10. God is all Powerful.* He is our Source of riches, honor, long life and help with enemies. Everything good comes from Him.
- *11. God can be pleased.* He was pleased with Solomon's request for wisdom.
- *12. God listens to us!* He asked Solomon what he wanted! He didn't just tell him what He wanted to give.
- *13. God is responsive to His children.*

"I have also given you what you have not asked"

1 Kings 3:13
(NASB1995)

Passage 4—God Is A Team Player (John 6:37-40)

John 6:37 "All that the Father gives Me will come to Me, and the one who comes to Me I will certainly not cast out.

John 6:38 "For I have come down from heaven, not to do My own will, but the will of Him who sent Me.

John 6:39 "This is the will of Him who sent Me, that of all that He has given Me I lose nothing, but raise it up on the last day.

John 6:40 "For this is the will of My Father, that everyone who beholds the Son and believes in Him will have eternal life, and I Myself will raise him up on the last day." (NASB1995)

FLCR FACTS

Jesus came down from heaven, not to do His own will, but to do the will of God the Father.

FLCR LESSONS

Christ was not coming to do His own plan, but was willing to leave heaven to do His Father's bidding.

FLCR CHALLENGES

Am I willing to do God's will, or am I focused on doing my own plan?

FLCR RESPONSES

Commentary

God the Father delegates. He shares His glory.

He sent Christ to do His will, but Christ did not mind. He had a good attitude. He was willing to leave heaven to do His Father's will because He trusted and loved God the Father and because He had an eternal perspective.

He didn't just focus on the temporary sufferings of this plan. He knew His sufferings paled in comparison with the eternal outcome for Him. He knew God the Father's plan would ultimately bring peace and fabulous blessings because His Father's plans always succeed.

How is your attitude? Are you willing to do God's will?

What God is Like

- 1. *He delegates.* He sent the Son to be our focus and His focus is on saving us and raising us up on the last day.
- 2. *God the Father does not need to be in the limelight.*
- 3. *God's plans work.* Anyone He sends to Christ will be received by Him.

"All that the Father gives me will come to me"

John 6:37
(NASB1995)

Passage 5—Facing Sin (2 Samuel 24:9-19)

2 Samuel 24:9 And Joab gave the number of the registration of the people to the king; and there were in Israel eight hundred thousand valiant men who drew the sword, and the men of Judah were five hundred thousand men.

2 Samuel 24:10 Now David's heart troubled him after he had numbered the people. So David said to the LORD, "I have sinned greatly in what I have done. But now, O LORD, please take away the iniquity of Your servant, for I have acted very foolishly."

2 Samuel 24:11 When David arose in the morning, the word of the LORD came to the prophet Gad, David's seer, saying,

2 Samuel 24:12 "Go and speak to David, 'Thus the LORD says, "I am offering you three things; choose for yourself one of them, which I will do to you."'"

2 Samuel 24:13 So Gad came to David and told him, and said to him, "Shall seven years of famine come to you in your land? Or will you flee three months before your foes while they pursue you? Or shall there be three days' pestilence in your land? Now consider and see what answer I shall return to Him who sent me."

2 Samuel 24:14 Then David said to Gad, "I am in great distress. Let us now fall into the hand of the LORD for His mercies are great, but do not let me fall into the hand of man."

2 Samuel 24:15 So the LORD sent a pestilence upon Israel from the morning until the appointed time, and seventy thousand men of the people from Dan to Beersheba died.

2 Samuel 24:16 When the angel stretched out his hand toward Jerusalem to destroy it, the LORD relented from the calamity and said to the angel who destroyed the people, "It is enough! Now relax your hand!" And the angel of the LORD was by the threshing floor of Araunah the Jebusite.

2 Samuel 24:17 Then David spoke to the LORD when he saw the angel who was striking down the people, and said, "Behold, it is I who have sinned, and it is I who have done wrong; but these sheep, what have they done? Please let Your hand be against me and against my father's house."

2 Samuel 24:18 So Gad came to David that day and said to him, "Go up, erect an altar to the LORD on the threshing floor of Araunah the Jebusite."

2 Samuel 24:19 David went up according to the word of Gad, just as the LORD had commanded. (NASB1995)

FLCR **FACTS**

Joab gave the king the number of registered people in Israel and Judah.

41

FLCR LESSONS

God does not want us thinking our security comes from our own strength.

FLCR CHALLENGES

Is my security in God?

FLCR RESPONSES

Commentary

2 Samuel 24 starts with God being angry with Israel. Their security seems focused on the strength of their own military might. In *2 Samuel* they highlight their elite warriors. There is no mention of God. But, they won every battle because God enabled them. No wonder God was angry!

So He incites David's anger. He wants him to face his sin so he can get back on track. If David thinks his security is really with the troops, then face that, and go count them! David did not pause to consider his angry action. He did not ask God for wisdom. He just reacted and ordered the count.

It's a funny thing about making decisions when we are angry. The results are usually not satisfying. As soon as he received the number of troops he knew he had sinned. The number of fighting men was irrelevant. God was their security.

To David's credit he immediately went to God. He knew he had sinned and confessed his sin. He asked how he could atone for his sin, because he valued his relationship with God as more important than having it disrupted, no matter the cost.

God responds to confession. He wants to help David get back on track. It was important for David to realize his sin effected many people, not just himself. So God gave him three choices. If he was thinking about bearing the brunt of the consequences for his sin himself, he might have picked door 2—run from his enemies for three months. But, David realized his enemies were cruel and God is merciful, so he picked door 3—a plague over the land for three days. But, everyone would bear the brunt of his sin with that choice.

During the plague David sees that his sin has destroyed innocent lives so he asks God to allow him and his household to bear the consequences, alone. Finally, David has the right perspective, so God gives him a restorative job of building an altar to commemorate the end of the plague. Lesson learned. His security is in God, and his sin effects more than himself. God does not delay restoration when we get back on track. He is moved by genuine repentance.

David's reign is marked by incredible success, and terrible failure, but his strength is in his desire to keep his relationship with God pure. David shows us the virtue of humility and the destructiveness of pride, but that God remains faithful throughout.

What God is Like

- *1. God does not force us to do the right thing.* But, He wants us to face our sin to keep our relationship with Him pure.
- *2. God has emotions.* He was initially moved to anger, and then sadness as He saw the consequences of David's sin, and finally compassion as He accepted David's prayers and sacrifices.
- *3. God cares about His children.* He is intimately involved in our lives.
- *4. God responds to confession.* As soon as we get the right perspective He restores our relationship.
- *5. God wants us to feel better after we confess.* He gives us a way to do something constructive.
- *6. God does not hold a grudge.* He does not keep being insulted by our sin. He is moved by our prayer of confession.
- *7. God values His relationship with His children as important enough to suffer death.* He wants us to value our relationship with Him as equally important.
- *8. God has paid the price to secure His children's safety.* He wants us to live like we realize this.
- *9. God is powerful and wise enough to be flexible with us.* He can help us face things in many ways.
- *10. It grieves God to see the consequences of our sin.* He does not take pleasure in painful judgments.

- *11. God is secure.* He did not worry He would lose control if He incited David's anger. He wanted David to see the results of his sin.
- *12. God is holy.* He tells us how to atone for our sin. For David it was faith in God's forgiveness through animal sacrifice. For us, it is faith in God's forgiveness through Jesus Christ's sacrifice.
- *13. God is faithful.* He does not leave or forsake His children. He sees us through.

"Let us now fall into the hand of the LORD for His mercies are great"

2 Samuel 24:14
(NASB1995)

Passage 6—Help In Unlikely Places (1 Kings 17:7-16)

1 Kings 17:7 *It happened after a while that the brook dried up, because there was no rain in the land.*

1 Kings 17:8 *Then the word of the LORD came to him, saying,*

1 Kings 17:9 *"Arise, go to Zarephath, which belongs to Sidon, and stay there; behold, I have commanded a widow there to provide for you."*

1 Kings 17:10 *So he arose and went to Zarephath, and when he came to the gate of the city, behold, a widow was there gathering sticks; and he called to her and said, "Please get me a little water in a jar, that I may drink."*

1 Kings 17:11 *As she was going to get [it,] he called to her and said, "Please bring me a piece of bread in your hand."*

1 Kings 17:12 *But she said, "As the LORD your God lives, I have no bread, only a handful of flour in the bowl and a little oil in the jar; and behold, I am gathering a few sticks that I may go in and prepare for me and my son, that we may eat it and die."*

1 Kings 17:13 *Then Elijah said to her, "Do not fear; go, do as you have said, but make me a little bread cake from it first and bring [it] out to me, and afterward you may make [one] for yourself and for your son.*

1 Kings 17:14 *"For thus says the LORD God of Israel, 'The bowl of flour shall not be exhausted, nor shall the jar of oil be empty, until the day that the LORD sends rain on the face of the earth.'"*

1 Kings 17:15 *So she went and did according to the word of Elijah, and she and he and her household ate for [many] days.*

1 Kings 17:16 *The bowl of flour was not exhausted nor did the jar of oil become empty, according to the word of the LORD which He spoke through Elijah. (NASB1995)*

FLCR FACTS

The brook dried up.

FLCR LESSONS

We can be effected by God's judgment (no rain), but God takes care of His children.

FLCR CHALLENGES

Am I trusting God to take care of me as America gets judged?

FLCR RESPONSES

Commentary

God knew exactly where He wanted Elijah to go. He had already commanded the poor widow to help Elijah before Elijah knew anything about it. God cares about the details and He still has plans for His children. Sometimes His plans get very specific.

But, fasten your seatbelt, because His plans don't always follow our fallible logic. We would probably send Elijah to a rich household to find provisions. But God sends him to a sad, desperately poor widow. This way it is clear that God is the One Who is providing. The poor widow probably thought her life was worthless as she prepared to die. But God can use those who think they are "worthless."

Sometimes fear can be a stumbling block. It takes faith and trust in God to obey His unlikely requests. We might have to swallow our pride and ask for help from someone who is worse off than us. I'm sure as a poor widow no one looked to her for anything. But God noticed and spoke to her. He had a plan for her. She didn't really know God, but she obeyed Him.

Would you be willing to feed a stranger before your own child and yourself? She was. It was a good choice because God has command over flour and oil! He did not ask her to find spare coins under the couch cushions so she could go buy more. He just kept making more flour and oil.

Elijah and the widow were both effected by God's judgment on their sinful nation. We can also be effected by God's judgment on our own sinful nation. In their case there was no rain for years which diminished their water and food supply. But God takes care of His children and He is not limited by the effects of His own judgment. He can use a poor widow to take care of His own.

God might want us to ask for help in ways that defy logic. Or He might ask us to give help when we think we have nothing to give. It takes faith to follow God and watch Him work. If God can use the saddest, poorest widow to provide, He can use anyone, even us.

What God is Like

- 1. *He is powerful.* He has control over a poor widow's flour and oil.
- 2. *God wants us to know He is the One taking care of us.* So He provides miraculously.
- 3. *God can use the saddest, poorest widow to accomplish His will.* It is never too late for anyone.
- 4. *God can use someone who doesn't really know Him to help accomplish His will in our life.*
- 5. *God is in the details of our life.* He had a specific plan for how He would provide for Elijah and the widow.
- 6. *God's judgment on a sinful nation can effect His children, but He cares and has a plan to provide for His own.*
- 7. *God is not limited by our limitations.*
- 8. *God wants us to have faith in Him when He defies our human logic.* Sometimes we have to obey when it isn't logical.
- 9. *God sees value in the poor and needy.*
- 10. *God can supply our needs from what looks like impoverished sources.*
- 11. *God wanted to use the poor widow when everyone else thought she had nothing to offer.* He cares about the least of us.

Passage 7—God's Broad Shoulders (Ezekiel 36:21-32)

Ezekiel 36:21 "But I had concern for My holy name, which the house of Israel had profaned among the nations where they went.

Ezekiel 36:22 "Therefore say to the house of Israel, 'Thus says the Lord GOD, "It is not for your sake, O house of Israel, that I am about to act, but for My holy name, which you have profaned among the nations where you went.

Ezekiel 36:23 "I will vindicate the holiness of My great name which has been profaned among the nations, which you have profaned in their midst. Then the nations will know that I am the LORD," declares the Lord GOD, "when I prove Myself holy among you in their sight.

Ezekiel 36:24 "For I will take you from the nations, gather you from all the lands and bring you into your own land.

Ezekiel 36:25 "Then I will sprinkle clean water on you, and you will be clean; I will cleanse you from all your filthiness and from all your idols.

Ezekiel 36:26 "Moreover, I will give you a new heart and put a new spirit within you; and I will remove the heart of stone from your flesh and give you a heart of flesh.

Ezekiel 36:27 "I will put My Spirit within you and cause you to walk in My statutes, and you will be careful to observe My ordinances.

Ezekiel 36:28 "You will live in the land that I gave to your forefathers; so you will be My people, and I will be your God.

Ezekiel 36:29 "Moreover, I will save you from all your uncleanness; and I will call for the grain and multiply it, and I will not bring a famine on you.

Ezekiel 36:30 "I will multiply the fruit of the tree and the produce of the field, so that you will not receive again the disgrace of famine among the nations.

Ezekiel 36:31 "Then you will remember your evil ways and your deeds that were not good, and you will loathe yourselves in your own sight for your iniquities and your abominations.

Ezekiel 36:32 "I am not doing [this] for your sake," declares the Lord GOD, "let it be known to you. Be ashamed and confounded for your ways, O house of Israel!" (NASB1995)

FLCR FACTS

God the Father has concern for His holy Name.

FLCR **LESSONS**

God will allow His Name to be profaned for a period of time, but He vindicates the holiness of His great Name at some point.

FLCR CHALLENGES

Do I worry that God's Name is profaned, or do I realize He will vindicate His holy Name at some point?

FLCR RESPONSES

Commentary

God the Father must have broad shoulders. His children abuse and disrespect His Name and He patiently waits for the appropriate time to vindicate the holiness of His great Name. He is not anxious or insecure about the slander. He knows Who He is. Eventually all will know. But for now, He puts up with the abuse while He executes His plan.

He has made promises that He will keep because He is good, not because we are good.

In this passage, He reminds the nation Israel that they are His people even though they have profaned His holy Name in front of the others nations. God says He will do what it takes to vindicate His Name.

Apparently, it will take a lot.

He has to cleanse Israel from all their filthiness and idols by giving them a new heart and spirit so that they will obey Him. Then He will give them the land He gave to their forefathers and cause the land to multiply with fruit and produce. He is not helping them for their own sake, but to vindicate His holy Name so that the other nations will know that He is the holy Lord God. He wants everyone to know Him as the only Lord God. He has the power to tell the grain to increase or decrease!

He hates to tell it to decrease. He wants to be known as Israel's One-and-only-holy-God who provides abundantly. But, Israel profaned His Name when they turned to idols and sin to meet their needs instead. For their own good, He cannot bless that.

It is a good thing that God is willing to fix everything. All He asks is for Israel to recognize their evil behavior and have remorse because they slandered Him with their sin and idols. This will speak volumes to the nations around them. They will notice when Israel throws out their idols and repents of their sin. This will honor His holy Name. He wants children who want to obey Him and feel remorse and shame when they don't. He vindicates His Name so all will have a chance to recognize Him as the only true God.

This seems to be the pattern for us as well. God has provided the ultimate solution for us through Christ. He just wants us to recognize our evil behavior, repent, and obey Him. This communicates to those around us that God is a holy God. When we live in sin and refuse to obey God we profane His Name so others don't recognize Him as a holy God. In order to vindicate His Name He sent Christ so we could have a new heart and spirit. God is the One Who helps us because of His holy Name, not because we deserve His help. Our obedience reverences His holy Name to those around us.

What God is Like

- 1. *He is patient.* He waits to vindicate His Name.
- 2. *He is not an anxious leader.* He does not worry that His Name is being slandered for a while. He knows He will vindicate His Name.
- 3. *He cares about everyone.* He wants us to obey and reverence His holy Name so that all will see He is Lord God in our lives.
- 4. *He likes to bless His children.* He wants to bless our obedience so others will know that He is the Lord God.
- 5. *He wants His children to be ashamed and embarrassed by their sin because our sin keeps those around us from recognizing His holy Name.*
- 6. *He does not want His children to feel disgraced by famine.* He wants to bless His obedient children because it shows others He is the only true, great, holy God.

Passage 8—Love Your Enemies (Matthew 5:43-48)

Matthew 5:43 "You have heard that it was said, 'YOU SHALL LOVE YOUR NEIGHBOR and hate your enemy.'

Matthew 5:44 "But I say to you, love your enemies and pray for those who persecute you,

Matthew 5:45 so that you may be sons of your Father who is in heaven; for He causes His sun to rise on [the] evil and [the] good, and sends rain on [the] righteous and [the] unrighteous.

Matthew 5:46 "For if you love those who love you, what reward do you have? Do not even the tax collectors do the same?

Matthew 5:47 "If you greet only your brothers, what more are you doing [than others?] Do not even the Gentiles do the same?

Matthew 5:48 "Therefore you are to be perfect, as your heavenly Father is perfect. (NASB1995)

FLCR **FACTS**

You have heard: Love your neighbor.

FLCR **LESSONS**

God loves His enemies and treats them well. He wants us to be like Him.

FLCR CHALLENGES

Am I willing to follow God's example and be like Him with regard to an enemy?

FLCR RESPONSES

Commentary

God does not react in kind.

If we are mean and selfish He does not get punitive and act mean and selfish back to us. His love governs His behavior even when He is angry or is disciplining us. He never sins. God treats His enemies well. They get His sun and rain.

Is this a blank check for your enemies or are there limits? God the Father loves His enemies, but He has certain boundaries. There are times when He puts an end to evil. How can we tell when we are acting like God in our patience with evil treatment or when we should say "enough" and flee?

God seems to judge evil when the burden of the evil is too great for His children to bear. I don't think this passage means a woman should stay with a violent husband until he beats her to death. Or that missionaries should willingly stay with captors who plan on killing them. If evil is enough to overwhelm and destroy, it is time to flee if you can.

The attitude you maintain after you flee is the issue. Do you love your enemy because God loves them? Do you pray for them? Do you want to be like God who loves and forgives despite our behavior?

God offers a reward for those who are willing to follow His lead to love instead of seeking revenge. If we imitate God's love and acceptance for our enemies, that is behavior God describes as *perfect*.

It may sound like loving your enemy is weak. But loving your enemy is not being a doormat—it is not *passive* love—it is *active*. If you are actively praying for, and finding ways to help, that is different than being a doormat who passively puts up with abuse.

When the evil behavior threatens safety you don't stay and enable it. It is loving to flee before their out of control behavior kills or seriously injures someone. It also gives the abuser a wake up call.

What God is Like

- *1. God the Father is generous.* He is willing to share His love and blessings with both the righteous and the unrighteous. He offers a reward to those who follow His lead and love instead of hate.
- *2. God the Father wants to help all His children.* Even those who work against Him. He wants us to be like Him and help those who persecute us by loving and praying for them.
- *3. God the Father is not impossible to please.* He calls our behavior "perfect" if we are willing to love and pray for people who do not deserve it.
- *4. God the Father is perfect.* He loves and helps all His children, even though we don't deserve it. He gives all His children love. He provides sun and rain for all and allows everyone the freedom to choose Him.

"He has made promises that He will keep because He is good, not because we are good."

the Authors

Appendix A
Answers

More answers are given below than you are expected to find when you study the passages. Most people find four to six *Facts,* one or two *Lessons,* one or two *Challenges,* and one *Response* when they study a passage. Extra answers are given here to help you better recognize *Facts, Lessons, Challenges,* and *Responses.*

1—He Includes Us (Exodus 3:9-22)
Facts
- God hears the cry of the sons of Israel.
- God has seen their oppression by Egypt.
- God said He would send them to Pharaoh.
- So that Moses could bring My people (the sons of Israel) out of Egypt.
- Moses said "who am I to go to Pharaoh to bring sons of Israel out of Egypt?"
- God said "certainly I will be with you" and I'll give you a sign:
- After you bring them out of Egypt you will worship me at this mountain.
- Moses asked what name to call God.
- God said I AM WHO I AM so say I AM has sent me to you.
- God said to tell them "the LORD, the God of yours fathers, the God of Abraham, the God of Isaac, God of Jacob has sent me to you.
- God said this is His Name forever.
- God said this is His memorial name to all generations.
- God told him to gather the elders of Israel together and say the God of your fathers, the God of Abraham, Isaac and Jacob has appeared to me and I am indeed concerned about you and what has been done to you in Egypt.
- God said to tell them He will bring them out of the affliction of Egypt to the land of the Canaanites, Hittite, Amorite, Perizzite, Hivite and Jebusite to a land flowing with milk and honey.
- God told Moses they will listen to him.
- God said Moses should go with the elders to the king of Egypt and tell him the God of the Hebrews has met with us so let us go on a 3 day journey into the wilderness to offer sacrifice to God.
- God said he won't let you go except under compulsion.
- God said He would strike Egypt with miracles until he lets them go.
- God said He would grant the Israelites favor with the Egyptians.
- God said they would not leave Egypt empty-handed.
- God instructed every woman to ask her neighbor and every woman living in her house to give her silver, gold and clothing.

- God instructs the women to put the plunder on her sons and daughters.
- God said this would plunder the Egyptians.

Lessons

- God is aware of His children's suffering and is concerned. Sometimes He allows it to last a long time for His own reasons.
- Sometimes God asks us to go directly to our enemy and negotiate.
- Sometimes God has to compel a person to comply with His will.
- We focus on ourselves, but God wants us to focus on Him.
- God foretells the future and gives a sign to look forward to when He asked Moses to do a scary thing.
- God's Name says He is complete and in the moment.
- God wants His children to have abundance.
- God can grant us favor with our enemy.
- God can use trials to influence His will.
- Sometimes God's will involves asking for what you want. He gives favor, but we have to ask.
- God is able to redistribute wealth.
- Things can look hopeless. The Israelites were slaves and oppressed and then God turned the tables and oppressed them. They left Egypt rich.
- God cares about our children. He wants to provide for them.
- God does not force His will. He just made Pharaoh miserable until he chose God's will. There is God's sovereignty and man's responsibility again.

Challenges

- Do I take comfort that God is aware of suffering but has a purpose?
- Would I be willing to negotiate with an enemy if God asked me to?
- Am I willing to comply with God's will so He doesn't have to compel me?
- Am I focused on God or myself as I follow Him?
- Do I take enough advantage of God's Word foretelling the future in these scary times?
- Do I take comfort in God's Name?
- Do I believe God wants abundance for His children?
- Have I asked God to give me favor with an enemy?
- Is God using a trial to accomplish His will? Is there some way I need to be cooperating?
- Am I willing to ask for what I want if God instructs me to?
- If God is willing to give favor, am I willing to ask?
- Do I trust God to redistribute wealth according to His will?
- Am I willing to have hope even when things look hopeless?
- Do I take comfort that God wants to provide for my children?
- Do I trust God to lead me?

Responses
- Father, thank You for being aware of our suffering.
- Thank You for caring.
- Thank You for having a purpose and plan for us.
- Thank You for the hope that You can turn things around and give us favor and provide for us and redistribute wealth.
- Thank You for abundant provision.
- Please help us do your will.

2—Asking For Reassurance (Judges 6:34-40)
Facts
- The Spirit of the LORD came upon Gideon (verse 34).
- He blew a trumpet.
- Gideon told the Abiezrites to follow him.
- Gideon sent messengers throughout the land (verse 35).
- Men of Manasseh, Asher, Zebulun and Naphtali came to join him.
- Gideon talked to God.
- He told God if He really had promised to deliver Israel through him,
- He wanted to test what God had said.
- Gideon told God he would put a fleece of wool on the threshing floor.
- If there was dew just on the fleece, and the floor was dry, he would know he understood that God would deliver Israel through him.
- It was so.
- The fleece was wet enough to fill a bowl full of water. The floor was dry.
- Then Gideon asked God to not let His anger burn against him,
- He asked to speak again.
- He asked for one more test with the fleece.
- He asked that the fleece would be dry but the floor would be wet with dew.
- It was so.
- The fleece was dry and the ground was covered in dew.

Lessons
- God can equip us to do His will, and we can still need reassurance.
- God seems patient with our insecurity when we are endeavoring to obey Him.
- God can use insecure/flawed people to show His power.
- God lets us ask for more reassurance, in order to work with our weakness.

Challenges
- Am I willing to believe that God will equip me to do His will?
- Do I worry God will get mad at me if I'm endeavoring to do His will, but I want some reassurance?
- Do I think I need to be perfect for God to use me?

- Do I worry that God won't work with my weakness?

Responses
- Father, thank You for using weak and imperfect people to display Your great power and grace.
- Thank You for equipping us with what we need to do Your will.
- Please forgive me when I just focus on myself and worry I can't do Your will.
- Please forgive me when I focus on myself and think I can do Your will myself.
- Your grace and kindness to include Your flawed children in your victories is amazing.
- May I always obey Your will. It is always better than anything I could ask or think for my life.
- I don't want to get to heaven and discover I missed doing Your will for my life because I was insecure, instead of secure in You.

3—Asking For Wisdom (1 Kings 3:1-14)

Facts
- Solomon formed a marriage alliance with Pharaoh's daughter.
- Pharaoh was king of Egypt.
- Solomon brought Pharaoh's daughter to the city of David.
- He was still building his own house, the LORD's house, and the wall around Jerusalem.
- People were still sacrificing on the high places.
- The temple had yet been built.
- Solomon loved the LORD.
- He obeyed the laws his father David had taught him.
- But Solomon offered sacrifices and burned incense at the high places.
- Solomon went to the city of Gibeon to offer sacrifices.
- That was where the most important high place was.
- He offered 1,000 burnt offerings on the altar there.
- The LORD appeared to Solomon at Gibeon.
- That night, during a dream, God told Solomon to ask for anything he wanted from God.
- Solomon answered: you have been very kind to my father David, Your servant.
- Solomon said God had been faithful to David because David had been faithful to Him.
- Solomon said David did what was right with an honest heart so You have continued to be very kind to him.
- You have given him a son to sit on his throne today.
- Solomon acknowledged that God had made him king in David's place.
- But, Solomon said he was a little child who didn't know how to carry out his duties.
- He told God he was His servant,
- serve great people that are too many to be counted.

- He asked God for an understanding heart so he could judge between good and evil.
- He acknowledged no man could judge God's people.
- God was pleased with Solomon's request.
- God said because Solomon had not asked for a long life, or riches, or death for his enemies, but instead discernment for justice,
- God agreed to his request.
- He gave Solomon a wise, discerning heart,
- Wiser and more discerning than anyone before or after him.
- God also gave him what he didn't ask for:
- Riches and honor above all other kings all his life.
- God told Solomon if he kept obedient to His commandments as David did, he would prolong his life.

Lessons

- We don't have to be perfect to be blessed by God. God saw that Solomon was humble and loved Him and wanted to obey Him.
- David and Solomon both loved God so they (imperfectly) obeyed His commandments.
- God loves His children coming to him humbly asking for wisdom.
- You can't out-give God. God was moved by Solomon's obedient, extravagant, burnt offering, so He told Solomon He could ask for whatever he wanted.
- Sometimes God uses dreams to speak to us.
- God responds with loving kindness and blessings for those who walk in truth, righteousness and a loving heart towards Him.
- We can sin, but if we have a sincere, honest heart towards God we get back on track with Him.
- God is the One Who can bless our life even after we die.
- We are going to need God's help to do His will. He wants to join us in enabling it.
- We are all God's servants here on earth.
- God wants to bless His loving, obedient children.
- God is abundantly generous. He didn't just make Solomon wise, he made him wiser than anyone before or after him.
- God can bless us the most if we keep sincere and loving hearts towards Him all our life.
- God can give provisional promises based on our behavior. He doesn't promise to keep blessing evil behavior.

Challenges

- Do I realize God looks at my loving heart towards Him and not just if I occasionally sin?
- Do I obey God's commandments because I love Him?
- Do I realize I need God's wisdom enough to ask Him for it regularly?
- Do I ever extravagantly give to God out of gratitude?
- Do I pay attention to vivid, unusual dreams?
- Do I walk in God's truth with righteousness and a loving heart?
- When I sin do I see it as a heart issue before God and endeavor to

be humble and repentant before Him to restore my heart?
- If I want my life to have meaning after I die am I loving and obeying Him?
- Do I admit I am inadequate to do God's will so I ask for His help?
- Am I living like God's servant?
- Do I think God wants to bless me?
- Do I see how abundantly generous God was with a sincere, loving, obedient Solomon?
- Do I love and obey God so He can pour out all the blessings He wants?
- Am I doing anything that hinders God's blessings on me?

Responses
- Father, thank You for being such an extravagant Giver!
- Thank You for being powerful enough to give wisdom, honor, riches, long life and sovereignty over enemies!
- Thank You for being flexible and kind with my attempts to love and serve You with my whole heart.
- Thank You that You can be pleased with my fallible attempts to live for you.
- Thank You for wanting to love and help me as I endeavor to serve You.
- Thank You for asking Solomon what he wanted! You are Father God of the universe listening to fallen man!
- Thank You for wanting to help and enable me!
- Please forgive me when I get distracted.

4—God Is A Team Player (John 6:37-40)

Facts
- Everyone the Father gives to Christ will come to Him.
- The one who comes to Christ I will never be cast out by Christ.
- Christ came down from heaven.
- Not to do His own will.
- He came to do the will of Him Who sent Him.
- This is the will of Him Who sent Jesus...
- ...Jesus will not lose one person that God gives Him.
- ...Jesus will raise them up on the last day.
- This is the will of God...
- ...Everyone who sees the Son and believes in Him will have eternal life.
- ...Christ will raise him up on the last day.

Lessons
- God the Father sent Jesus Christ to do His will. He delegates.
- Christ was not coming to do His own agenda, but was willing to leave heaven to do His Father's plan.
- God the Father sends people to Christ. This is Teamwork.

- Anyone God the Father sends will definitely come to Christ.
- Christ will not reject, or lose, anyone the Father sends Him.
- Everyone who sees and believes in the Son will have eternal life.
- It is the Son's job to raise believers up on the last day.

Challenges
- Am I willing to do God's will, or am I focused on doing my own plan?
- Am I taking comfort in the fact that Christ will never reject or lose me?
- Do I live my life like I know I have eternal life because I believe in Christ's work?
- Because I have eternal life, do I realize Christ will raise me up on the last day?

Responses
- Father, please help me to know Your heart and Your will and to do it.
- Thank you for saving me and for Your diligence to guard me and deliver me safely into eternity.
- Please help me to do Your will for my life.
- I want to please You.

5—Facing Sin (2 Samuel 24:9-19)

Facts
- Joab gave the King the number of registered people in Israel and Judah.
- There were 800,000 valiant men who could fight in Israel.
- There were 500,000 men in Judah.
- After David numbered the people his heart troubled him.
- David told the LORD "I have sinned greatly in what I have done."
- David asked God to take away his foolish sin.
- The next morning God sent the prophet Gad to spiritually advise David.
- God told Gad He was offering David three choices.
- He let David choose.
- Gad told David God was offering 3 choices...
- ...7 years of famine in the land,
- ...3 months of fleeing from his enemies,
- ...Or 3 days of pestilence in the land.
- Gad told him to decide and he would return to tell God.
- David told Gad he was in great distress.
- He decided to fall into the hand of the LORD because His mercies are great.
- David did not want to fall into the hand of man.
- The LORD sent pestilence upon Israel.
- It started that morning and lasted until the appointed time.

- 70,000 men from Dan to Beersheba died.
- When the angel stretched out his hand toward Jerusalem to destroy it, God relented from the calamity.
- He told the angel who was destroying the people "It is enough! Relax your hand."
- The angel was by the threshing floor of Araunah the Jebusite.
- David saw the angel striking down the people,
- David spoke to the LORD:
- I am the one who sinned,
- I have done wrong,
- But these sheep, what have they done?
- Please let Your hand be against me and my father's house.
- So Gad came to David that day.
- He told David to build an altar to the LORD on the threshing floor of Araunah the Jebusite.
- David did just as the LORD commanded.

Lessons
- God does not want us thinking our security comes from our own strength.
- Our anger can incite foolish sin, which we deny at first, but as soon as we complete the sin we know we were sinning.
- David's pure relationship with God was more important to him than avoiding consequences, so he faced his sin with God.
- God is flexible. He does not have only one way to deal with our sins, or one timeline.
- God is responsive to confession. He gives us something to do so He can bless us again.
- When David realized his sin was hurting those around him, he asked for punishment against himself, and his household. Then God gave him something constructive to do to atone.
- We tend to think our sin only effects us. God wants us to know there are always consequences for the ones around us when we sin.
- We can be innocent and yet destroyed by the consequences of someone else's sin.
- God demands justice for sin. Now Jesus is the justice for our sin.
- God may cause us to face our sinful way to help us turn from it.

Challenges
- Is my security in God?
- When I am angry, am I willing to withhold any action until I'm no longer angry?
- Is restoring my relationship with God more important than avoiding pain?
- Am I grateful that God is flexible with me?
- Have I thanked God for being so responsive to confession?
- Do I see that God wants to help me after I confess sin?
- Do I think my sin is only effecting me?
- Do I realize innocent people get destroyed by another's sin?

- Have I thanked God that Jesus provides the justice God needs for my sin?
- Do I have any sinful choices I need to face and confess?

Responses
- Father, thank You for being my security.
- Please forgive me when I worry about my security in this evil world.
- Thank You for being sovereign and for Your love never failing.
- Thank You for caring enough to help me face any sin and get back on track.
- Please forgive me for thinking my sin only effects me.
- May I have Your wisdom and patience to withhold any action while I am angry.
- I don't want my sin to hurt innocent people around me.
- Father, may I always value my relationship with You as more important than avoiding the pain of consequences. You are my security and my source of love, joy and peace.
- Thank You for being so responsive to my confessions because of Jesus.

6—Help In Unlikely Places (1 Kings 17:7-16)

Facts
- The brook dried up.
- There was no rain.
- God spoke to Elijah.
- God told him to go to Zarephath, part of Sidon.
- He told him to stay there.
- God told Elijah He had commanded a widow to provide for him.
- Elijah went to Zarephath.
- He saw a widow gathering sticks at the city gate.
- Elijah said "please get me a little water in a jar to drink."
- As she was going to get it he said "please bring me a piece of bread in your hand."
- She said it was true she had no bread like it was true Elijah's God lives.
- She said she only had a handful of flour in a bowl,
- Plus a little oil in a jar.
- She told him she was gathering the sticks to prepare a meal for her son and her to eat before they die.
- Elijah told her not to fear.
- He told her to do as he said,
- But to make him a little bread cake first.
- He told her to bring it out to him first.
- Then she could make one for herself and her son.
- Then Elijah told her what God told him:
- The LORD God of Israel will not let the bowl of flour run out,

- Nor shall the jar of oil run out,
- Until the LORD sends rain on the earth.
- So she did what Elijah asked.
- She and her household ate for many days.
- The bowl of flour and jar of oil did not run out,
- Just as the word of the LORD said through Elijah.

Lessons

- We can be effected by God's judgment (no rain), but God takes care of His children.
- God's divine provision can come from a very unlikely source (the poor widow).
- God can use someone desperately poor to share and be hospitable.
- We need faith to follow God's direction for our provision.
- Sometimes God's will isn't logical by man's standards. We would send Elijah to a rich person's house.
- God might ask us to ask for help where we don't want to. We will need faith in Him to obey.
- God might ask us to give help when we don't think we can. We will need faith in Him to obey.
- God wants us to trust and obey Him. He has a plan.
- The widow listened to God even when she was not sure Who He was. God can talk to, and use, anyone.
- God can use the weakest, saddest person to accomplish His will.
- God cared about the sad widow getting ready to die.
- God cared about Elijah, His servant, who was relying on Him for his survival.
- Sometimes God wants us to obey Him before tending to our family and ourselves. He promises to meet our needs that way.
- God does not want us to fear as we obey Him.
- God keeps His Word.
- Sometimes God has very specific directions for where He wants us to go.

Challenges

- Am I trusting God to take care of me as America gets judged?
- Do I appreciate that God can supply my needs from what looks like impoverished sources?
- Would I be willing to let someone desperately poor share with me and be hospitable?
- Do I trust God to take care of me?
- Do I expect God's will to fit my logic?
- Would I trust God's plan if He asked me to get help from someone worse off than me?
- If God asked me to share and give help when I am desperate myself would I be willing?
- Do I trust God's plan for me?
- Am I thankful God notices the poor and those who don't really know Him, but He can use and help them?

- Do I appreciate God's power, that He can use the weak and powerless to accomplish His will?
- Do I realize God cares about a sad widow who didn't really know Him, but was getting ready to die?
- Do I also see God was caring about His servant Elijah and meeting his needs?
- Would I be willing to obey God if He asked me to meet the needs of a stranger before the needs of my family and myself?
- Am I willing to obey without fear because God knows what He is doing?
- Do I live like I know God keeps His Word?
- Am I willing to follow God if He gives me very specific directions?

Responses

- Father, thank You that Your ways are beyond our ways.
- Thank You that You are not limited by our limitations.
- Thank You that You can use a sad, desperately poor widow to do Your will.
- Please help me to recognize Your will and follow Your way. I want to follow You and trust You when You ask me to do something that doesn't follow man's logic.
- It is wonderful to watch You accomplish Your will.
- Thank You for letting me know and follow You.
- Thank You for taking care of me.

7—God's Broad Shoulders (Ezekiel 36:21-32)

Facts

- God the Father has concern for His holy Name.
- Israel profaned (abused, disrespected) His Name everywhere they went.
- Therefore, God told Israel He was about to act, not for their sake, but for His holy Name.
- God will vindicate the holiness of His great Name which they profaned among the nations.
- Then the nations will know that I am the Lord God Who proves Himself holy among Israel so the other nations see.
- God will take Israel out of the nations and give them their own land.
- He will cleanse them from their filthiness and idols.
- He will give Israel a new heart and new spirit within them.
- He will remove their heart of stone and replace it with a heart of flesh.
- He will put His Spirit within them and cause them to obey His statutes and ordinances.
- Israel will live in the land God gave to their forefathers.
- Israel will be God's people and He will be their God.
- God will save Israel from all their uncleanness.
- He will call for the grain to multiply.
- God will prevent famine.

- He will multiply the fruit and produce.
- Israel will not have the disgrace of famine among the nations.
- Israel will remember their evil deeds and loathe themselves.
- God is not helping them for Israel's sake.
- Israel should be ashamed and embarrassed by their behavior.

Lessons
- God will allow His Name to be profaned for a period of time, but He vindicates the holiness of His great Name at some point.
- Many times God tells us what He is going to do before He does it.
- God will bless us even when we don't deserve it because He is holy and keeps His promises.
- God cares how we represent Him by the choices we make to obey or disobey Him.
- God can cause famine or great abundance. Can you imagine the power it takes to tell the grain to decrease or increase?
- God wants us to be ashamed and embarrassed by sinful behavior because it means we don't care about Him and His holy Name. He can help us start over with a new soft heart and spirit within that chooses to obey Him.

Challenges
- Do I worry that God's Name is profaned, or do I realize He will vindicate His holy Name at some point?
- Do I profane God's holy Name by disobedience?
- Do I take the time to read God's Word so that I know what is going to happen?
- Do I believe that God keeps His promises?
- Do I believe that He will bless me based on His promises?
- Do I realize I am representing God by the choices I make to obey or disobey?
- Do I realize God can cause famine or great abundance where I live?
- Am I ashamed and embarrassed when I choose to sin and thereby profane God's Name?
- Do I go to God when I sin and allow Him to help me start over with a new heart and spirit?
- Am I asking God to help me choose to obey Him?

Responses
- Father, thank You that You have broad shoulders and that You are patient with our sin.
- Please forgive me when I represent Your holiness in my life.
- Please help me keep my heart soft and honor You.

8—Love Your Enemies (Matthew 5:43-48)

Facts
- You have heard: Love your neighbor.
- You have heard: Hate your enemy.
- But I say...
- ...Love your enemies,

- ...And pray for those who persecute you.
- So that...
- ...You may be sons of your Father in heaven.
- He causes His sun to rise on the evil and good.
- He sends rain on the righteous and unrighteous.
- If you love those who love you what reward do you have?
- Don't tax collectors do that?
- If you greet only your brothers how are you doing more than others?
- Don't Gentiles do the same?
- Be perfect like your Heavenly Father is perfect.

Lessons

- God loves His enemies and treats them well. He wants us to be like Him.
- God wants us to love, bless, do good, and pray for our enemies while they hate us, curse us, despitefully use us and persecute us.
- There is an implied reward for this behavior...
- It is perfect behavior to be loving when you are being abused.
- God the Father behaves differently than the world around us. He wants us to behave like Him, even if it means our behavior won't conform to the world we live in, or seem fair to us.
- God the Father wants us to love everyone, including our enemies. He wants us to pray for those who persecute us. Then we will be acting like Him.
- God the Father wants to reward us for behaving like Him, instead of trying to fit in with the world by only accepting the people who treat us well.
- God loves all His children. He even loves the ones who work against Him as His enemy. He does not immediately judge them. He keeps sending His love, sun and rain on them.
- God is perfect. He wants us to look at how He treats us and behave like Him.
- God wants us to stand out and be different from Gentiles.

Challenges

- Am I willing to follow God's example and be like Him with regard to an enemy?
- Am I willing to love someone who is trying to hurt me?
- It is a very active response. Am I willing to take the initiative or will I be a doormat just passively putting up with abuse?
- Can I focus on the reward?
- Am I willing to be perfect in this behavior or immature?
- Do I believe my enemy needs my love more than revenge? Can I trust God to sort it out?
- Do I want to be like God or like the abuser?
- Do I behave like the world around me, or like God the Father?
- Am I willing to be different?
- Am I willing to love and pray for my enemies?
- Do I want God's reward for behaving like Him, or would I rather

blend into the world and seek revenge?
- Am I willing to love my enemies, even if they mistreat me, because God loves them?
- Do I realize if I imitate God's love and acceptance for me with my enemies, I will be behaving like Him and God calls that kind of behavior perfect?

"Love your enemies."

Matthew 5:44 (NASB1995)

Printed in the USA
CPSIA information can be obtained
at www.ICGtesting.com
LVHW090419201024
794251LV00001B/89

9 780979 159572